Built by Love, Kept by Grace:
Beauty out of Ashes

All scripture references, unless noted otherwise, are from the Holy Bible, King James Version.

All rights reserved. No part of this book may be reproduced in any form without permission in writing from the publisher/author, except in the case of brief quotations embodied in church related publications, critical articles, or reviews.

Printed in the United States of America
ISBN 978-1-7375503-0-3

Copyright © 2021 by Quatina Frazer

Cover design and photographs by Quatina Frazer

Published by Quatina Frazer
qfrazer@gmail.com

Dedication

I believe that this book can and will inspire both men and women; however, mothers were on my heart as I thought about writing this book. Because of that, this book is dedicated to mothers, whether single, married, or divorced.

This book is also dedicated to my sons who have endured many things right along with me. They have had to go without certain things because I could not provide them as a single mother; they have had to go without me as I sacrificed extra time to work or to go to school, and they have had to go without me as I dealt with physical pain, depression, and trauma throughout a large part of their childhood.

I believe the scripture that says, "They overcame by the blood of the Lamb and by the word of their testimony" (Revelations 12:11); therefore, I have authored this written testimony to continue to overcome and to inspire others to overcome.

Contents

Dedication	i
Preface	iii
Chapter 1 - The Breaking	1
My Beginning	1
My Childhood	2
Adolescence to Adulthood	7
Chapter 2 – Wounded, But Willing	11
The Hard Truth	11
Resilience	18
Chapter 3 – The Son Comes in Mourning Time	24
Ain't No Sunshine When She's Gone	24
'Til Death do us Part?	27
Chapter 4 – Development on the Journey	33
Identity	33
Introspection	36
Triggers	42
Personal and Professional Development	43
Intentional Living	44
Chapter 5 – Diamond in the Rough: Hidden Gem	46
Life Goes On	46
God is Able	48
Mindset Shift	50
Hidden Gem	51
Acknowledgements	54
About the Author	55
Bibliography	56
Pending Book Titles	57

Preface

Life is a sum of choices. Our life either goes in the direction of our own choices or in the direction of the adult figures' choices in our lives. My story begins with the latter.

In the beginning of this book, I briefly describe my childhood and how it played a role in setting up the mindset that I carried as I began to make decisions for myself. Even though I was loved fiercely by my family and had experienced God's love, I made decisions that reflected little love for myself. This book shares some of the trials as well as the triumphs of my life, and the lessons I have learned along the way.

To the person reading this book, I pray that you be infused with hope and the revelation that God is real and that He loves His creations, including YOU! As God did with me, He can redeem you and turn things around for your good. All you have to do is make a choice; choose Him and choose life!

Chapter 1 - The Breaking

"For I know the thoughts that I think toward you, saith the Lord, thoughts of peace, and not of evil, to give you an expected end."

~Jeremiah 29:11

My Beginning

If you knew me as a little girl, you would know me as a quiet little thing (according to me; my late maternal grandmother would say otherwise). Matter of fact, you would probably know me as my brother's sister. He was much more outgoing than I was and made friends very easily. I knew many people in my community because of the large family that I was a part of, but I really only had a handful of friends. I was born in New England, in the small state of Connecticut. My immediate family moved around a lot. I went to five of my town's elementary schools and spent two years in South Carolina attending two of their elementary schools. I believe that the frequent moves contributed to my social awkwardness and the development of anxiety. The introverted personality that I developed protected me at times, but it also kept me, I believe, from a more fulfilling life experience.

Vulnerability takes wisdom and courage, and I found myself choosing to be alone rather than risk opening myself up to other people. This theme of closing myself off would continue as I reached my breaking point, and if I am honest, it can easily be a crutch today. In fact, it has taken me many years to write this book; not because I did not have the time per se, but because of the fear of being vulnerable, exposed, and judged, coupled with feeling that my voice was not relevant and therefore would be rejected.

Unfortunately, self-sabotage had held power over me. I think it was a coping mechanism to lessen any possible future blow of pain or disappointment. In fact, I had to actively fight against the negative thoughts and feelings I had before I could produce this book and attain my goals.

My Childhood

During most of my childhood, we lived in "the projects." I do not believe that the projects that I lived in were as bad as large inner-city projects or neighborhoods may have been (my mother and

> *Vulnerability takes wisdom and courage, and I found myself choosing to be alone rather than risk opening myself up to other people.*

grandmother were born in North Philadelphia); however, the environment definitely influenced my personality and how I looked at the world. For example, I was afraid to travel anywhere that was not familiar. In middle school, I made it to the finals in the Spelling Bee competition. Do not judge me too harshly, but regrettably, I misspelled a word on purpose due to fear. I was afraid of traveling to Washington, D.C. That is how strong fear was in my life. Self-sabotage won that battle.

As with anything, there were positives and negatives in the way that I grew up and in the places that I grew up. In fact, I did not realize that I had grown up below the Federal Poverty Level (FDL), "poor," until I was well into adulthood. I knew that my family could not afford certain things, but I did not equate that to being poor.

Both sides of my family have history in Connecticut, my maternal side more than my paternal side; therefore, I grew up being around my mother's family for most of my childhood and life. My maternal side of the family was very close and helped each other whenever possible but was not very affectionate in my recollection. I knew that I was loved fiercely by my immediate and even extended family, but the love was shown more in action than stated in words. The lack of verbal expressions of love, as you can imagine, made future relationships, especially romantic relationships, challenging. There is a book called *The Five Love Languages* by Gary Chapman. It is interesting that my top love language is Words of Affirmation, which I feel I lacked growing up. Words have always been a part of my story in one way or another. From the time that I was a little girl, if I was not singing, I was writing. If I was not writing songs, I was writing poetry. In addition to that, I would keep words around my home on walls or decorative items, and I would wear them on clothing.

We often reciprocate love the same way we received it or how we want to receive it. There are people who love gifts and the way that they show love is to give gifts. When I was younger, I expressed love through action because that is how it was modeled for me. Even though I still do acts of service for people to express care and love, the way that I show love now is mostly through words. I lend my voice to love, encourage, and inspire those around me and those in my social media following.

I distinctly remember the time where I began telling my children that I loved them. I am a little ashamed to say that at first, it was a little awkward, but I am so happy that it has become normal. I cannot go without telling my sons that I love them. This life is so short, and we never know when the Lord will call our name.

Not having much affection physically or verbally expressed growing up also contributed to my hesitation to express affection toward God. I was not used to lifting my hands or doing a dance, but even more so, I was not used to saying, "I love you." When I should have been pointing my attention and affection to God, I was looking for love in all of the wrong places.

Growing up, my father was in and out of jail and my life. In hindsight, I can see where this created a desire for male attention and other negative attributes. I had received inappropriate male attention from a young age, and unfortunately, I was even the victim of molestation. The difference with my story, unlike many others, is that I was not exactly sure who had molested me, as the person thought that I was asleep. Being touched inappropriately and receiving flirtatious comments from older men, all led to trust issues within me. I did not tell my father (or anyone) what had happened to me because I did not want to be the cause of him returning to jail. As I think about it now, that experience is a lot for a little girl to carry alone. The first person to know what had happened to me was my husband at the time, and I told him after we were married; it was buried so deep. I do not remember what triggered the memory, but that release was long overdue.

Adolescence to Adulthood

The irony is, later in life I desired the attention. I had unknowingly tied it to value and worth. I was not invincible and unnoticeable any longer when I received the attention.

One effect of accepting the attention I received is that I became a teen mom at the age of 16. The suggestion of abortion was presented to me, but because of my Christian upbringing, I knew enough to know that abortion was wrong; therefore, I chose to keep my son. My convictions were deep rooted.

Not only did my maternal grandmother help to keep us in church when we were very little, but my paternal grandfather was also a reverend and a pastor. In fact, there were and are individuals in the ministry on both sides of my family. As I got older, my mother became more serious in her walk with Christ. We would have Bible study in our home, not just with immediate family, but she would invite children from the neighborhood to join in as well. I did not appreciate that act of love and service to God back then as much as I do now.

Church has been a part of me ever since I can remember. I also have always loved music and the two combined are heaven on earth to me. I had my first solo in the church around the age of 6 or 7 years old. I sang, "Jesus is the Answer" with a childhood friend in the children's choir. I do not recall singing another solo until I was in my late teens or early twenties. That introverted and fear-filled personality hindered me from pursuing anything serious with singing. I never entered any type of talent show or contest. I would sing in my school chorus or the background of my church's choir but never lead. I could not risk messing up or being embarrassed. The enemy of God wants to keep us so full of fear that we never live out our dreams or more importantly, our purpose and calling.

"Surprisingly," I became a teen mom twice over. After the school administration let me back into high school, I had to withdraw again and finish my studies at the town's Adult Education Center. I began attending adult high school with my maternal grandmother. You see, she was a teen mother as was my mother. My grandmother was the motivating force behind me and said that we could finish together. I graduated along with my maternal grandmother in the year 2000. Generational patterns are very real. I was pregnant with my second child when I graduated high school, and my mother had me, her second child, in her belly when she graduated high school.

At 15, I had dated my second son's father briefly, then we broke up and I became pregnant with my oldest. About a year later, we got back together, and I became pregnant again. My father said, "The first time was a mistake. The second time, you knew what you were doing." I would never call any of my children a mistake, but I knew what my father was trying to say. He was right. I felt that I was in love. I was young and naive and said, "No one else is going to have your babies."

I was only 19 years old when we got married and my ex-husband was from another country. I am sure you can imagine the strain from many directions on our young family and marriage. As you will discover in the coming chapters, pain, devastation, and even selfishness took me to places that I never intended on going.

I concluded that even though I did not want to admit that I had been broken, I had been. Yet, like the master potter that He is, God took my broken pieces from each circumstance and period and began constructing a beautiful mosaic. I could not see His construction at the time, but hindsight has shown that He has worked all things together for my good. I thoroughly believe that nothing has been wasted and that what I do not understand presently, is yet to be revealed.

> *Yet, like the master potter that He is, God took my broken pieces from each circumstance and period and began constructing a beautiful mosaic.*

Later in life, I began to reflect and appreciate my pastor and church that I was in at that time because they did not cast me out for becoming a teen mother. I sometimes wonder how life would have been different had I been cast aside.

Chapter 2 – Wounded, But Willing

"And He went a little farther, and fell on His face, and prayed, saying, O my Father, if it be possible, let this cup pass from me: nevertheless not as I will, but as thou wilt."

~Matthew 26:39

The Hard Truth

In the early years of my marriage, I answered a call into the ministry. Over time, it seemed that as I was getting closer to God, my husband was drifting further from God. After eight years and after trying to make it work, I filed for divorce. I struggled with filing for divorce because, once again, I was a Christian and I was now a minister. The Bible says that God hates divorce; however, I had to come to peace within myself about it. Only then could I move forward.

I will not go into too much detail regarding my ex-husband. I will allow him the opportunity to tell his own story or testimony, should he choose to do so, but I will share some of what I endured. I also want to say that it takes two people to make a marriage work and that there were many things that we did not know and mistakes that we both made. Forgiveness and grace are a part of the healing process. Not only did I have to forgive him and those involved in my pain, but I also had to forgive myself. I am sharing not out of bitterness, but I am sharing out of hope for the betterment of someone else. If I can climb out of my shell of pain and begin to heal from such devastation, I ask what can God do for another? At the end of a healing journey, and sometimes even during it, you come to realize that people are just mere flawed human beings, and my father and my husband were no different.

One day, I had a conversation with a woman in ministry who was a prophetess, and during the conversation, she mentioned a few things to me that led my husband and me to have lunch with her. By this time, we had known her for several years, so I trusted her word and counsel. After lunch, on the drive home, I asked my husband what I felt my gut and spirit already knew. He confirmed that he had had an affair. Disbelief and devastation both hit me at once. Before I got married to him, there were other women and drama that had occurred, but we were saved and married now. I did not start out "right," but I tried my hardest to make it right. I knew that I had children out of wedlock, I had apologized to another woman for my part in her pain, I had gotten serious with Christ, I did not want to "shack up" and fornicate, and so I got married, and I answered a call into the ministry. What else could I do to "make it right?"

The sad thing about this time was that I not only felt that my ex-husband had let me down, but I also felt like God had let me down as well; although I never wanted to admit this to myself or even admit it out loud. I served Him with all of my strength. We were encouraged as a couple for our faithfulness to the church and our sacrifice of time and energy. How could this happen? How could I not see the signs? Moreover, why had God not prevented this from happening?

This pain and divorce were not in the plan! In fact, when I first got married, I stated that I would never use the word divorce. Even though healthy relationships and marriages were scarce and not evident around me, I did not grow up and dream of this outcome! I did not say, "When I grow up, I am going to get divorced and I want my children to grow up without a father consistently present in their lives." I thought what was happening to me was completely unfair. This was NOT what I had signed up for! Even before the divorce, I had to experience consoling my toddler children, my sons, often explaining to them that daddy was not coming home. There were times where I had to figure out where my car was or use a lock on the steering wheel. There were times where I had to get money from my "husband" through a third party. Times where I left notes at places where I knew he would end up, just to communicate with him, all very painful and humiliating. And just when I thought I could not become anymore wounded, creativity kicked in and I would have a fresh wound.

> *During this season of great trial and pain, I learned what it really meant to be a worshipper.*

During this time of brokenness, I felt as if everything either had stopped or should have stopped. Life was just going on and I was struggling to function. I could not bring myself to pray. During this season of great trial and pain, I learned what it really meant to be a worshipper. One phrase that came to me at that time was, "When I'm at my lowest point, I'll give God the highest praise!" I learned how to praise and worship in and through the pain, and that act of sacrifice and worship helped carry me through to healing. I was not totally silent though. When I could not pray, I would sing and write songs. I understood that the word is powerful and that if I could just keep the word in my spirit, that I would be okay eventually. And when I could not sing, I would just cry. I would not wish pain like that on anyone. The pain of a broken heart. I knew at that moment how it could kill someone. I had comfort in the fact that the Bible says that God not only bottles our tears, but the Holy Spirit also intercedes on our behalf with our groans when we have no words to say.

Not only did I worship, but I also kept attending church, no matter how sporadic it seemed. I kept hearing the quote "Tie another knot and hang on!" ringing in my ears! A preacher that I once knew talked about his addiction and said that he just kept going to church, no matter what. As I stated in Chapter 1, isolation was not abnormal to me; however, one Sunday when I missed service, some of my cousins and young women from the church came to my home to pray with me and encourage me. That act of love meant the world to me. The encouraging words were instrumental in my healing process. Death and life are in the power of the tongue.

If you take nothing else away from this chapter, take away the fact that people need encouragement and hope! My late cousin would often encourage me, and it was not just during the divorce; she and her husband helped counsel my ex-husband and me when we first got married because they were married at a young age also.

People who genuinely care and who pray and not gossip are so needed and are so invaluable. I distinctly remember days where individuals came up to me and asked me boldly about MY BUSINESS, even in front of my young children. I could not, for the life of me, figure out why God would allow this open shame. I felt like the whole town knew about what was going on with my marriage and household and I had to sit on the pulpit through it all. I am very much a sensitive soul as much as I am a stubborn princess; many Sundays, my feelings and emotions were on display, whether I wanted them to be or not.

During this time, I still had to serve, give, preach, sing, work, and educate myself to pull my family out of poverty. I still had to MOTHER my children. When I tell you that God's grace carried me through, I absolutely mean every word of it. When people get to know me, they sometimes say that they are amazed at all that I have overcome. They cannot comprehend that I am amazed as well!

Family was critical during this challenging season. My mother, grandmother, sister, aunts, and many others were so helpful with my sons. My older cousin helped with the haircuts of my four young men. Unfortunately, I could not rely on their father to cut their hair, help pay for cuts, or even bring them to the barbershop during the time of separation and divorce. I felt so out of place, but my cousin made sure that I felt welcomed at his barbershop *and* that I had a seat. I will be forever grateful for the family and friends that took my sons to events when I could not. I am thankful to those who gave clothes to my sons, came to my home, and helped me by giving discipline and advice to my sons.

I realized that I could not be a father. I could raise my sons to the best of my ability to be good people and gentlemen, but I could not teach them to be a man.

Resilience

Filing for divorce was one of the toughest decisions of my life, especially having four sons at the time ranging from ages 4 to 11. In 2005, I began the journey of higher education, taking after my mother. She was the first of my grandmother's children to obtain a college degree. There were times that I wanted to quit college, but something would not let me give up or give in! I had reasons now; my sons were my reasons! I had to succeed for them, I had to be an example for them, and I wanted them to go further than me.

When I first began college, I recall receiving notice from the State Department that in order to continue receiving food assistance, I had to end my studies. As terrified as that decision was, I rejected the idea that I had to stop attending college. I wanted to pull my family out of poverty, and I believed that education would help me do that. I wanted to get out of the cycle so many find themselves in.

I started college very strong academically. I was pleasantly surprised at this because I had no intention to go to college while I was younger. Something clicked for me and I think it was the fact that I was there not because I "had to be" per se, but because I wanted to be. I had a goal in mind and reasons to help propel me toward the finish line.

I worked in the Admissions Office and they began to know that I would be getting A's in my courses. As time went on and my life became increasingly challenging with a divorce looming, my grades became slightly lower. Thankfully, this did not stop my membership in the community college's chapter of the International Honor Society. I was inducted into the honor society and I also served as secretary for a year.

I graduated in 2008 with my associate degree. I received numerous scholarships and awards, and I was a part of the All-CT Academic Team. The team consisted of one student from each of the 17 community colleges in the state. This achievement granted us a ceremony at the State Capitol. I transferred to a state university after graduation. Although I did very well my first semester, I made the decision not to continue attending at the large physical location. It was very challenging attending the university being a single mother of toddlers and having health conditions. However, I did not give up! I ultimately completed my bachelor's degree online at my state's public online college and I finished with honors! I am thankful to God for His grace and to my family for the many times they stepped in to help my sons and me through those years.

Someone once said to me before I finished my bachelor's degree, "Look, you went to college, and where has it gotten you?" Those words hurt and could have made me say, "They're

> *What will you choose to do with the options you have been given or the situations that you have created?*

right! What am I doing? Who do I think that I am?" I am so glad that I did not quit!

What will *you choose* to do with the options you have been given or the situations that you have created? I could have thrown in the towel because of my health alone. From a young girl to that present time, I had suffered from digestive issues, headaches, and migraines, pancreas issues, and because of pregnancy, I later had heart issues. Imagine working, taking care of toddlers, going to school, operating in ministry, and on top of that, having recurring health issues. My physical ailments not only caused frustration, but also contributed to depression.

I was wounded in so many areas, not just physical issues of the heart, but emotional wounds as well. I had so many excuses I could have used to quit, but grit would not let me! Being wounded and still deciding to operate with grit and being willing to push forward is what separates those who achieve success from those who settle for less. I took a quote by Dr. Martin Luther King Jr. to heart. It says, "If you can't fly, then run, if you can't run, then walk, if you can't walk, then crawl, but whatever you do, you have to keep moving forward."

I was determined to crawl to the finish line, sobbing and all! Another quote that helped me along the way is, "We must embrace pain and burn it as fuel for the journey," stated by Kenji Miyazawa. These quotes, in conjunction with my faith and my "reasons," my sons, provided the motivation and inspiration for me to keep fighting forward.

When I felt that I had lost my passion, hope, and joy, reciting scriptures became incredibly important for me. Psalm 51:12 says, "Restore unto me the joy of thy salvation; and uphold me with thy free spirit." I needed my joy back; I needed a willing spirit and I needed to be sustained.

Purpose also fueled me. The scripture says, "And we know that all things work together for good to them that love God, to them who are the called according to His purpose" (Romans 8:28). His purpose is about the kingdom of God. God would have that none should perish. I believed that my overcoming would help inspire someone else to keep going (not just going forward aimlessly, but with purpose), to overcome, and to believe in God. Not only that, but my overcoming would build the foundation for generational blessings because of obedience and sacrifice for God.

No matter where you find yourself, I pray that you do not give up. Time continues to pass anyway. Keep fighting forward, making strides toward your purpose and calling in life. Find your reasons, find another reason to "tie another knot and hang on," and most importantly, find God. Seek out His will for your life and yield to it.

Chapter 3 – The Son Comes in Mourning Time

"But unto you that fear my name shall the Sun of righteousness arise with healing in His wings; and ye shall go forth, and grow up as calves of the stall."

~Malachi 4:2

Ain't No Sunshine When She's Gone

"The Son Comes in Mourning Time" was a message that was inspired within me shortly after I lost my maternal grandmother. I so desired for her to be healed. I believed and prayed and had faith, and all of that was shaken when her health began to rapidly decline. Not only did I lose my grandmother, but my marriage had also been unraveling for some time at that point. I felt that I had no support from the person I needed most, my then-husband.

I must have been looking up scriptures on healing to have come across Malachi 4:2. I just remember the words rearranging in my mind. The scripture says, "...the Sun of righteousness..." but I saw the Son as in "Son of God." The sun rises in the morning. Well, my grandmother passed early one Sunday morning. I stayed with her until her last breath. It was hard for me to leave her bedside, hard for me to leave the hospital room, hard for me to leave the hospital, and most certainly hard for me to leave the cemetery.

It was hard for the human part of me, even though my spirit knew she was no longer in any of those places, including her own body. She was with the Lord. I grieved so deeply. Because I was with her a lot from a young age, she was the grandparent that I was the closest to. I even looked like her, sang like her, and at times walked like her. How could she be gone?

I needed comfort and healing. The message "The Son Comes in Mourning Time" was definitely a message that God spoke to my heart for ME! As I mentioned before, the maternal side of my family was not very affectionate, but my grandmother expressed her love in many ways. I remember being rushed to the hospital from work for an abdominal pain that I was having. My grandmother met me at the hospital. She was rubbing my back and even said, "I love you!" I believe that was the first time that I had ever heard those words come out of her mouth. I got really nervous and thought to myself, "Something serious must be wrong with me!" It just turned out that I had an inflamed pancreas and that I was pregnant. I chuckled to my grandmother and said, "Look at the bright side, I'm married this time!" Needless to say, she didn't find it amusing.

My grandmother cared deeply for her family and evidence of that was seen in her many prayer books and index cards where she prayed specific prayers on our behalf. She had a hum that she was known for. I believe that helped her stay peaceful and even maybe connected to God more, singing and making melody in her heart.

After her death, it took me almost two years to begin to feel "normal" again. After experiencing that level of loss and grief, I was determined never to think about there being a proper amount of time to grieve again. Everyone is different and therefore everyone processes things differently. May we commit to being there for others without judgment as they go through their journey of healing.

Interestingly enough, even though my faith had been shaken by her illness and death, it was my faith that carried me through to healing. There are questions that I may never know the answer to, but I trust and believe God through it all.

As I reminisce and write about her, I remember why we grieve. We grieve because the person we love so much will no longer be with us in physical form. We grieve, not only because we are human, but also because love transcends this world, and it never dies. As long as there is breath in our bodies, we could and should still feel that love.

'Til Death do us Part?

Not only did the Son come in the time of me mourning my grandmother's death, but the Son also came while I was mourning the death of my marriage. The marriage had unfortunately died long before the actual divorce date. I once heard Dr. Myles Munroe say something like, "Divorce is worse than the death of a spouse." From what I understood, Munroe was saying that it is very difficult to grieve the loss of someone that is still alive. I cannot agree or deny either way because I have never experienced the death of a spouse, but I can say that divorce feels very deathlike.

Whoever said marriage is just a piece of paper lied. Even after the divorce was final, initially, the feelings and situations for the most part remained. I could not figure out for the life of me why we could not just be done with each other. Why did I have to feel this pain? Why did I have to experience this shame? Why did my oldest son have to now "lose" two fathers? Why did I have to continue with this drama from other women?

I mourned the loss of what should have been! That might be the worst pain. To think about all of the future events and milestones that were supposed to take place. The dreams and visions were now null and void, as was the marriage in a sense.

Holidays and birthdays had always been tough toward the end of the marriage, but even more so after the divorce. To spice things up, I would get a call from the police station or a knock at the door to give me some news! I did not understand why the news always seemed to come around some significant day that I was supposed to be enjoying.

> *In fact, my compassion for others grew out of journeying through and surviving my own pain.*

All of this felt incredibly unfair! What kind of person deserves so much disappointment and pain? I began to question myself. Wounded beyond measure, it was as if I was in an extended season of mourning for one reason or another. A vicious cycle of shock, bitterness, and depression.

During this time, I even recall venting on social media a lot. I felt like I was not being seen OR heard! Well, someone was going to hear or "read" what I had to say! Having gone through a period of such pain, I rarely judge people who vent on social media. I am not saying that all should get a pass. I am just saying to give a little more grace because until you have experienced the depth of someone's hurt or pain, you cannot understand why they do what they do. In fact, my compassion for others grew out of journeying through and surviving my own pain.

I felt that no one truly understood my pain. No one cared about my happiness! My children were too young to even know to care about certain needs that I had. My ex-husband was never around to care or see the damage he had done and continued to do.

There are many lessons that I take from this period of my life, one being "Don't become the person that hurt you!" I began to change into someone other than myself. I began to act in ways I would have never acted, do things I would not normally have done, and I did not care who I hurt or who was not happy because I was not happy. If we are not careful, pain can turn us into the very people we say we do not want to be like.

There is a scripture that states, "But every man is tempted, when he is drawn away of his own lust, and enticed. Then when lust hath conceived, it bringeth forth sin; and sin, when it is finished, bringeth forth death" (James 1:14-15). At times, I would use this scripture against my ex-husband. There was no room for, "The devil made me do it!" I thought and said, "No! The Bible says it right here, you were drawn away because you wanted to be!"

Me saying that to him also begged the question for myself later: Why did I do the things that I did? Was it because the devil made me do it? Was it because of pain? Was it because it was simply what I desired, and the situation was the perfect breeding ground and excuse for me to go ahead and do it?

That scripture in James is so powerful and I try to keep it ever before me now. We do not sin because grace abounds. I want to remember the very real evolution that could happen from one choice. This is also why we must be mindful about what we meditate on and desire and lust after because if we are not strong enough, we will act on those thoughts, and when fully conceived, death occurs.

I found myself meditating on my pain, on the people who hurt me, on my revenge, and on what I had lost. I was leaving little

> *God heard beyond my words and interpreted my cry.*

room for God, no room for positivity, and no room for healthy love.

I thank God that He did not leave me nor forsake me in my time of brokenness, pain, bitterness, and straight-up rebellion. He KEPT me when I did not want to be kept. He did not hold my bitterness against me. It is almost like he saw past what I was saying and doing and saw my broken heart. Thank God for the blood of Jesus!

Have you ever seen a baby whining, crying, and trying to convey something to its parents? Through my pain, groaning, and moaning, God deciphered what I felt, and He began turning things around. He heard my cries for mercy. God heard beyond my words and interpreted my cry. The Bible tells husbands to dwell with their wives with understanding (1 Peter 3:7). As a bridegroom, He gave me understanding. He covered me with His love, and I am forever grateful. He came and picked me up just in the nick of time!

Chapter 4 – Development on the Journey

"If ye then be risen with Christ, seek those things which are above, where Christ sitteth on the right hand of God. Set your affection on things above, not on things on the earth. For ye are dead, and your life is hid with Christ in God. When Christ, who is our life, shall appear, then shall ye also appear with him in glory."

~Colossians 3:1-4

Identity

I was at my wit's end, in despair when God came and rescued me. Please do not mistake me, I believe that He was there with me all along, but God is not going to force us to take His hand. From the beginning of time, He has been a God of free will. Those of us who love Him do so because we freely choose to. He did not make angels or people as robots, so although I believe that there is a longing within humanity to worship something or someone, God desires us to love Him of our own free will. I believe that is true love. This is one reason why I do not believe that God chooses our spouse for us. Love chooses! I do believe, however, that He gives us wisdom, discernment, and guidelines to help us make the right decision.

When I got married at 19, I do not believe that I did so for the best reasons. I made a choice to marry, and I was in love, but I lacked wisdom, as I was very young, and I did not have many resources or examples as models. Therefore, when my marriage began to unravel, more of my identity unraveled with it. It seemed inevitable as I did not have a proper identity growing up.

I was mourning the loss of my marriage when I should have also been mourning the loss of myself. Who was I now that I was not married? To take it even further, who was I outside of being a young mother? What did Tina like? What were Tina's goals? Did I have an individual purpose?

I did not know who I was. From the time that I could remember, I had put everyone else's needs before my own. There was a level of service and love behind it, and at times religion played into it, yet fear and rejection often played a bigger part. It was a pattern and it played out even if the service or love action negatively affected my well-being.

What I really should be saying, although it is difficult to admit, is that I was a people pleaser. There are several signs of people-pleasing such as not wanting to say no, wanting to avoid conflict, not admitting when your feelings are hurt, feeling responsible for how other people feel and more (Morin, Psychology Today).

> *As I think about some of the signs, I know exactly why I became a people pleaser, and that was to lessen the trauma.*

As I think about some of the signs, I know exactly why I became a people pleaser, and that was to lessen the trauma. I did not want to experience a barrage of harsh words, words that cut deeply through the mind, soul, and spirit, all in one shot. I did not want to feel invisible and sometimes I felt that I could only be heard or seen if I was a mirror for someone else. I did not want to involuntarily experience physiological responses (nausea, anxiety, upset stomach). I did not want to cause disappointment or anger or see it displayed through facial expressions and passive-aggressive behavior. I did not want to wonder what was wrong with me. Lastly, as much of an introvert as I was, I really did not want to be alone. Loneliness felt too close to abandonment, which also felt close to rejection.

Introspection

There came a point in my life where I chose to put labels and stigmas aside and I realized that it would probably be a good idea if I talked to someone, so I began to search for a therapist. I credit being in community with others for this realization. I had gathered with some women for lunch, and one had disclosed that the way she had empowered herself for the women's holiday we were celebrating was to find a therapist. After that lunch meeting, I believe several of us were empowered to do the same. She recommended Psychologytoday.com, and I now recommend the site as well. It was very user-friendly and easy to filter through to locate a potential candidate.

As I mentioned previously, I grew up in a Black, Christian family. Although I loved God and I did spiritual things, I knew there was a part that I was neglecting. I was neglecting to confront an unstable childhood, sexual violations, and emotional trauma.

> *I needed some help to unpack, inspect, and decrypt the experiences that I had gone through and I needed steps to mental and emotional wholeness.*

Again, I am not saying that my childhood and life were all bad; however, I needed some help to unpack, inspect, and decrypt the experiences that I had gone through, and I needed steps to mental and emotional wholeness. I wanted to dig deep and to find out the reasons behind not only my behaviors but also my thought processes.

I remember when I first met my therapist. I chose a woman and more specifically, a woman of color. I did not want her to be an atheist per se, but I did not mind if she was not a Christian. In fact, I did not want her to be "overly" Christian. I had real issues and drama and I did not want to hear, "Just pray about it."

During our first meeting, she asked me if I had experienced any trauma. I thought about it and I said, "Hmmm, no, I have not." After about 3 sessions in, she said, "Tina, I need to talk to you. When I first met you, I asked the question if you had experienced any trauma. Your answer was "no," but you have described almost nothing but trauma, and you gloss over it as if it is nothing!" I do not know if I cried or not in that moment, but

> *How many of us "gloss over" pain and trauma?*

I feel like crying right now. How many of us "gloss over" pain and trauma? As a Black woman, I can say that I have felt that I had to be strong no matter what. I had to carry my weight and the weight of those who were not handling their own responsibilities. I had to handle my weight with grace. Many things happen to us from childhood to adulthood, and many times, we do not have the answers that we need, nor do we process what we have experienced. Often, we do not even have the language to articulate what has happened or how we feel. We hold it in, we suck it up, and we keep it moving! I do not believe that I am the only black woman who feels that if I do not always function, that EVERYTHING would fall apart! I could only sustain this high level of functioning for so long. It became imperative for me to seek out help.

I also want to say that as I sought out a counselor; I encouraged my sons to do the same. Things that happen in the home typically are not singular in who they affect; what affects one affects another. My sons and I would have infrequent, in-depth conversations about the past, and they would reminisce. I would be in disbelief about how much "stuff" they remembered.

> *Trauma was not supposed to enter their world and become their reality.*

One day, I laughed and chuckled with them, but right after, I went to my room and cried. Again, my sons did not deserve this. Trauma was not supposed to enter their world and become their reality. I decided to file for divorce. I wanted to shield them from any further distress and protect them from what I had partly experienced while growing up. I felt that five lives were in grave danger and that we could not afford to risk life and future for one person who was being reckless. I thought about my sons' futures, and I thought about my future, if I decided to stay in the marriage. I was spiritually dying. I was letting myself go; I was making unwise choices concerning the places that I would go to look for my ex-husband. I mean, I did some stupid things. I said to myself, "I have to let this man go before I lose everything." It was to that degree, so therapy was long overdue.

Therapy helped with familial and romantic relationships as well as coming to terms with the past. There are still times when the past tries to rear its ugly head, but I can see my growth in dealing with situations that arise and I am much quicker to be self-aware and to be held accountable for whatever reaction I may have. I strive to learn and grow from every situation, good or bad.

To help me with my anxious thoughts, my therapist would give me exercises or ask me questions that would provoke me to think and dig deep. She also gave me coping techniques to help me in certain situations. I remember one trip that I was going on and I was so anxious. She told me to pack what I needed to so that I would feel secure and at ease. That might seem like a little thing to someone else, but I felt free after that to go ahead and overpack my little travel backpack. I had something in my backpack for any emergency that could arise, and I felt good about it.

My therapist asked me tough questions like, "When are you going to care what about Tina wants? When will you stick to the healthy boundaries you set and know what you deserve and need? When are you going to have that tough conversation and make the move that is best for you?"

When I was not attending therapy, I would (and still do) go through seasons of journaling. I used to feel guilty seeing large time gaps in my journaling, but I have concluded that, for me, journaling is like an "as needed" prescription. I *could* write every night, but I do not need to; it is most beneficial to me when I have something internal that I need to release.

> *...journaling is like an "as needed" prescription.*

Therapy does not have to be a life-long commitment. I learned that I could go as little or as much as I needed or felt comfortable with. It was nice to be able to speak about issues and feelings and get feedback without bias. This time was well spent, and the results were invaluable.

Triggers

As you are growing and developing on your journey, you may be in situations or around individuals that may cause something to be triggered within you. Sometimes the questions the therapist would ask me would trigger a painful memory that I had forgotten. Other times, situations with a significant other would cause me to react irrationally because something within me was triggered (or something within them).

Initially, it could take a tremendous amount of effort to be self-aware. Have you ever had to catch yourself in the middle of an argument, better yet, have you ever had to catch yourself before the attitude and argument began? We have a choice of how we react to our present situation or information. It is a wonderful feeling to be able to recognize growth in oneself. "Do the work!" I believe that it will be as worth it and as rewarding to you as it has been for me. And if you have an off day, give yourself grace. I have tried to make it a practice to give myself the same grace and compassion I give others when they need it.

Personal and Professional Development

Development, personally and professionally, internally and externally, became increasingly important to me. I began to look for ways to grow in character, communication, and confidence.

One of the things that I have come to find challenging is dealing with an individual who is not self-aware. I have always had a sense of personal accountability, but with more knowledge comes greater accountability. I am a life-long learner; it is just a part of who I am and my personality. Because of that, I want to examine my own heart and check myself before anyone else has to check me. This has helped not only to mature me but also to build my character.

For the most part, the training that I took part in at work could be applied in my home life as well as on the job. One training, in particular, Crucial Conversations, impressed me the most. It gave me the tools that I needed to begin having critical and important conversations. The biggest lesson that I learned from the training is that we tell ourselves a story, and we react based on the story that we told ourselves. This revelation has helped me to be more understanding when conversing, and it has helped me to be clearer in expressing my message.

Growing in communication and confidence has given me the desire to work toward healthy boundaries in my relationships and connections. I encourage anyone and everyone to take time to invest personally and professionally in themselves.

Intentional Living

I began giving myself something to look forward to and something to work toward. I could not keep waking up, going to work, paying bills, and being a mommy (chef, chauffeur, etc.) without having goals and pleasure built in. When I began my job about 10 years ago, I even remember having to use my vacation time for my sons. If I had a day off during the week, rarely was it for personal enjoyment.

> *Living with faith and intention gave me the strength to endure daily life.*

Hobbies and enrichment experiences became a part of my life and became intentional. I voluntarily went to workshops, conferences, and seminars. I also planted a garden for a few years, I took guitar lessons for a little while (I need to take some more), I chopped off my chemically relaxed hair and "returned" natural while having fun learning different natural hairstyles, and I enrolled in graduate school, taking advantage of my employer's tuition benefit to ultimately obtain my master's degree.

> *Gratitude felt better than the attitude.*

I felt a difference when I chose to begin living with intentionality. Living with faith and intention gave me the strength to endure daily life. When I could not see past the day, I decided to take each hour, each minute, and sometimes each moment one at a time. I began to appreciate the simple things in life so much more. I am not perfect, and there were times that I still got upset or frustrated, but more often than not, gratitude felt better than the attitude.

Chapter 5 – Diamond in the Rough: Hidden Gem

"The Spirit of the Lord is upon me; because the Lord hath anointed me to preach good tidings unto the meek; he hath sent me to bind up the brokenhearted, to proclaim liberty to the captives, and the opening of the prison to them that are bound; To proclaim the acceptable year of the Lord, and a day of vengeance of our God; to comfort all that mourn; To appoint unto them that mourn in Zion, to give unto them beauty for ashes, the oil of joy for mourning, the garment of praise for the spirit of heaviness; that they might be called trees of righteousness, the planting of the Lord, that he might be glorified.

~Isaiah 61: 1-3

Gem: *A jewel; a precious or sometimes semi-precious stone cut and polished for ornament; something prized especially for beauty or perfection; a highly prized or well-beloved person (Merriam-Webster)*

Life Goes On

I would not say that I totally lost myself when my marriage ended, but I was very close. After experiencing divorce, I decided never again to put so much faith into a MAN and to instead have a world outside of a MAN. Man can and will fail you. Not even necessarily because he or she wants to, but just because as human beings, we are flawed. In addition, having a "world" outside of a man (or woman) will keep you not only

> *I must bring my happiness, as well as tools to maintain such peace and happiness, "to the table."*

balanced but also will keep you from becoming completely devastated to the point of no return.

Having balance also prevents the other person from becoming drained or from feeling responsible for your well-being and happiness. It is no one's responsibility to make or keep me happy. I must bring my happiness, as well as tools to maintain such peace and happiness, "to the table." I love the song "Pieces of Me" by Ledisi, but if someone asks me, "What is it that you bring to the table?", I do not want to say, "These are the pieces of me, take it or leave it!" I want to be ever-growing and striving toward wholeness. I do not desire to be in a deficit. I want to bring so much peace and happiness to the table that there are leftovers.

I had to determine that after divorce, and even after unsuccessful relationships post-divorce, LIFE GOES ON!

My life could not stop simply because a relationship had ended, or someone had left. My identity could not leave on the

> *I want to bring so much peace and happiness to the table that there are leftovers.*

coattails of another person. I had to learn who I was in all seasons and in all types of relationships.

It may take some time, as it has taken for me, for you to build yourself up to the point where it is okay for you to be alone. I am not talking about being lonely; I am talking about being alone. I had to ask myself, "Who am I when no one else is around?" Other questions I had to ask myself were: "Am I okay being alone?" "Do I like myself?" "Do I love myself?" "Would I date myself?" and so on. I began working on the person that I could be proud of, that my children could be proud of, and most importantly, that God could be proud of.

God is Able

When I sit back and reflect on my life, I can truly say that God is able. He is amazing and able to do more than we can think or ask, as the scripture says. God handled so many things that I did not even consider or think to ask. Do you know why? Because He knows what tomorrow holds.

I went from living in the projects growing up, to becoming a teen mother, to living in a different low-income housing unit as an adult, to becoming a divorced single mother of four. I graduated college with honors and after almost two years of being unemployed, I finally secured a full-time job with a flower company. When I got the full-time job, I received a phone call, an opportunity for a temporary position that would put me in the industry of higher education. By faith, I left that full-time position at the flower company and I accepted the part-time contract position. I again received word of a position at a local university and by God's grace, I got that permanent part-time position. Within the first year, my position changed to full-time, and I have been at my job now for almost 10 years.

What blows my mind, even more, is that 5 years into my position, my dependent tuition benefit became active, and my oldest son was a senior in high school. I did not have a cent saved for college let alone a cent in a savings account.

There were so many things that I had to learn and unlearn. I greatly lacked financial literacy. I often implore young people, including my own children, to gain wisdom in finances and to make wise financial choices. The financial struggles were not only due to being a single parent, but they were also due to being an ignorant consumer. The price for ignorance can truly be paid years and even decades later.

> *The price for ignorance can truly be paid years and even decades later.*

Mindset Shift

Living in low-income housing was not easy, but it was familiar. I only needed to worry about covering rent; however, my rent increased when my income increased. It was difficult to save. The poverty mindset also had me afraid to leave low-income housing. I was afraid of making too much and capping out of assistance. I was afraid of failing after moving and afraid of being evicted. I was also afraid of homelessness.

I had to work hard to overcome those fears and push forward in life and my goals. This is not to say that it was

> *God can support you even in the shift.*

easy, but this was said to hopefully inspire someone to take a leap of faith concerning a position or even a move. God can support you even in the shift. I remember being told that I would not be able to move into the location that I wanted. Well, I began collecting boxes anyway as if I were moving. Faith without works is dead; therefore, I was operating in faith, collecting and packing boxes as if I had received a "yes!" After about two or three months, I received a phone call saying that I had the go-ahead to move!

Hidden Gem

After a culmination of the experiences that I have had in my life, I realized something: I realized that I was special to God and that He cared about my well-being, and He cared about what concerned me. I understood that even though I had gone through dark, dirty, and hard places full of pressure, that it made me into a gem. People may have looked at me with a look of disapproval before, and some may even still, but I can tell you that I do not look like what I have been through. God's love built me back up and reconstructed me and His grace has sustained me.

My desire is to keep becoming. I want to be my authentic self and uncover more of my purpose in God. Real diamonds have flaws; a spotless diamond is a counterfeit. I have overcome much in life and it does not do me or anyone else any good to act as if I have it all together. Transparency and vulnerability are powerful when used correctly. Some of the most influential people who have touched my life (some that I know personally and some that I have never met) were open and honest about their struggles and about their pasts. I hope to inspire someone in like manner through this written account.

> *Transparency and vulnerability are powerful when used correctly.*

Remember that you are God's original. You are the original diamond and not a cubic zirconia copy. Our stories should inspire individual growth, not fuel a desire for replication. Each of us must endure our process and our own journey naturally. Did I want to avoid the processes of going through, growing, discovering, and healing? Of course! And I am still growing and healing! Nevertheless, in hindsight, I can see that the journey was fuller because of the process. A Christian rapper named Jahaziel said, "It's not the place that the journey takes you, it's the man that the journey makes you."

God has restored and continues to restore me physically, emotionally, spiritually, and financially. I am not where I used to be by any means. He has given me beauty for ashes. Where there was pain, there is now grace. Where I had shame, He covered me with His love. Who would not serve a God like that?

Acknowledgements

This book has been buried within me for some time; therefore, I would like to give thanks to those who helped to bring it to fruition. First, I would like to thank God for giving me the strength and courage to share my story. I would like to thank my family and friends who not only helped me with feedback at different stages of the process, but who also donated monetarily to produce this book. Finally, thank you to the individuals whom I did not know personally, yet who donated to this project. I am beyond grateful for the prayers, support, and donations received.

About the Author

Simply put, Quatina Frazer is a lover of Jesus! In fact, it is the love of Jesus that got Quatina through some of the toughest times of her life. Quatina feels that her experience in life from childhood to becoming a teen mother, to becoming a young wife and subsequently a single mother of four boys, gives her a unique and wide perspective when aiding teens and young adults. She holds an Associate of Science in Business Administration from Middlesex Community College (2008), a Bachelor of Science in Business Administration from Charter Oak State College (2011), and a Master of Arts in Liberal Studies from Wesleyan University (2020).

Quatina has a heart for the youth and a desire to see them walk in their full destiny by helping them avoid many of the missteps she herself has made. She also feels called to minister to single and divorced mothers. Quatina was licensed as a minister to preach in 2005, and later ordained as a reverend in 2013. Based in CT, she is currently an elder in her local church where she ministers the word of God. Quatina sings inside and outside of her church. Her first single, "You Did It Before (The Prelude)," was released independently in 2020 under the artist name Kwateena. Her desire is to cross barriers and to help create unity in the body of Christ. Only then, she believes, can the love, fruit, and gifts of the Spirit flow into the world in greater measure.

Bibliography

King James Version. Bible Gateway. Web. April 1, 2021.

Morin, Amy. "10 Signs You're a People-Pleaser." *Psychology Today*, Sussex Publishers, 23 Aug. 2017, www.psychologytoday.com/us/blog/what-mentally-strong-people-dont-do/201708/10-signs-youre-people-pleaser.

Pending Book Titles

Below are titles of books that Quatina has in her heart to complete in the future.

- The Unseen Giver
- Waiting on Morning
- In the Face of Fear
- Pieces and Remnants (Photo book)
- See Through Me (Photo book)
- Excavating Genealogy (Photo book)

www.ingramcontent.com/pod-product-compliance
Lightning Source LLC
LaVergne TN
LVHW051512070426
835507LV00022B/3068